BLESSED

FOR LIFE

God's Word of Blessing for You

David R. Schmitt

25 Devotions for Men

**The mission of CTA is
to glorify God by providing purposeful products
that lift up and encourage the body of Christ!**

because we love him.

www.CTAinc.com

BLESSED FOR LIFE

By David R. Schmitt
Copyright © 2009 CTA, Inc.
1625 Larkin Williams Rd.
Fenton, MO 63026

ISBN 978-1-933234-84-7
PRINTED IN THAILAND

The LORD *said to Moses, "Tell Aaron and his sons, 'This is how you are to bless the Israelites. Say to them . . . '"*

Numbers 6:22–23

> *The LORD said to Moses, . . . "This is how you are to bless the Israelites."*
> Numbers 6:22–23

I recently moved. Cleaning out the basement, I came across a box of memories. Artifacts from college. There, among the scattered pictures, was a letter from my father. I recognized his handwriting immediately.

Dad was forwarding some mail and asked me when I'd come home. That forwarded mail is long since gone. So is my father. But not the power of his handwritten words.

His words evoked memories. Dad steadying me on a bike as I rode down the driveway. Dad driving with me to college. Dad writing a letter, wondering when I'd come home. Though Dad is gone, I still have his words and, for a moment, remember the love and protection he offered in my journeys.

The Israelites were on the move. Again. Having been delivered from slavery in Egypt, it seemed that all they did was move. Pitching their tents in some patch of wilderness and taking them up again, they wandered for forty years through a desert. Yet, they were not alone.

God had given them his Word. A blessing. This God who could strike down the Egyptians with plagues, who could cover the morning ground with manna and fill the evening sky with quail—this God gave them his Word. With a powerful hand, he wrote blessings across the sands of the desert. He promised to be with them in all of their journeys and finally to bring them home.

God's blessing covers the highways and driveways of our world today, too. Our God is the Lord of all journeys. God the Father sent his only Son to lead you home. His road took him to hell and back to forgive your sins and to claim you as his own. In Jesus, he promises to watch over you. He rescues you when you wander, sets your feet back on his paths, and leads you home.

In these devotions, we will meditate on the blessing of God, seeing how he leads us step by step, giving us his blessing and promising his protection as we make our way home.

Jesus, you are the Lord of all of my journeys. Lead me every day, keeping me close to you. Amen.

OUR GOD IS THE LORD OF ALL JOURNEYS.

> *The LORD said to Moses, "Tell Aaron and
> his sons, 'This is how you are to
> bless the Israelites.'"*
> Numbers 6:22–23

In 1979, archaeologists uncovered bits of silver while excavating a burial site southwest of Jerusalem. Looking more carefully, they saw that these pieces of silver were miniature scrolls. It took three years to unroll them and to decipher what was written on them, but when they did, they saw the writing was of far more value than the silver. These scrolls contained the blessing of God.

Someone had inscribed the words of Numbers 6:24–26 on these miniature scrolls. What's more, the scrolls dated to the seventh century B.C.—the oldest biblical manuscript yet discovered.

The greatest treasure, however, is much older than this scroll. The promise of salvation dates back to creation! When Adam and Eve fell into sin, God promised to send a Savior. This Savior would crush the head of Satan and defeat the death that Adam and Eve had brought into the world when they sinned (Genesis 3:15). For years, people lived and they died, holding on to this promise.

One day, however, God wrote his promise in blood. In Jesus Christ, God became fully human. He took on our flesh. He was mocked, beaten, and crucified for our sins. Then his body was wrapped in cloths and buried in a tomb. Yet there, among the dead, God hid the world's most precious treasure: the blessing of eternal life.

On the third day, God kept his ancient promise. Jesus rose from the dead; no archaeologist will ever find his bones. Instead, those who trust in Christ find that even in the face of death, God still speaks his blessing.

Sometimes, it's hard to read the blessing of God in this life. Words like *cancer* and *stroke* loom large, while the fine print of God's blessing seems too small. Yet, God has claimed us as his own, his treasure! He will never leave us buried in the graves of this world. Jesus will come again to raise us and claim us as his own. That is God's eternal blessing spoken for you.

Lord God, in Jesus you have given me an eternal treasure, life everlasting. Help me to read your Word, hear your blessing, and value my life as a treasure from you. Amen.

GOD HAS CLAIMED US AS HIS OWN.

> *The LORD said to Moses, "Tell Aaron and*
> *his sons, 'This is how you are to bless*
> *the Israelites. Say to them . . . '"*
> Numbers 6:22–23

The Lord told Moses to tell Aaron and his sons to bless the people. Strange, isn't it? Couldn't God just have done it himself? Why did he have to involve people at all?

Of course, God could have blessed Israel without Moses, and certainly God *did* bless Israel without human help. But God also invited people to participate. This strange command tells us something about God: God involves people in his work of blessing.

The Talmud, an ancient record of Jewish law and history, tells us that when Aaron and his sons spoke these words over the people, they trembled. Holy awe filled their hearts because they knew God was working through them.

When do you experience awe like that?

A father holds his daughter in his arms for the first time. She's so small. Her eyes aren't open. She can't understand what he says, but he whispers something to her anyway. His voice trembles as he makes a promise: he'll do the best he can for her. He won't do everything right, but he'll do his best. This is a moment of holy awe. This father, in loving fear, participates in God's blessing.

God has placed people in our lives: a wife or children, friends or co-workers. God wants to bless these people, to protect and support them, in word and in deed, and he chooses to do this through us!

Just thinking about it makes us tremble! Can we really love one another as God has loved us? We are sinful, and too often we have strayed from God's ways. Like that father, sometimes it takes all our strength just to whisper a promise.

But God is the one working here. He chose this design, and he knows what he is doing. God sent his Son to forgive our sin, and by the power of the Holy Spirit he uses us to bless the lives of others.

As a father speaks to his child, so God the Father speaks to you today: "You are mine. You are blessed. Love others as I have loved you."

Holy God, bless me this day that I may be a blessing to others. Amen.

HOLY AWE FILLED THEIR HEARTS.

> *This is how you are to bless the Israelites.*
> Numbers 6:23

"The devil's in the details," he said, looking over the lease agreement. Whether reading the fine print of a contract or the small type of a sales ad, we've learned to live by this proverb.

Interestingly, the proverb originally said, "God is in the details." But over time, people stopped seeing him there.

Isn't that just how it goes sometimes? We look to God for the big picture but then rely on ourselves for the rest. We worship God on Sunday but then "take care of business" on our own the rest of the week. The devil is indeed in the details when we compartmentalize our lives, giving only a portion to God.

When the Lord gave his blessing to Moses, he focused on the details. He gave specific people specific words to speak. The Lord gave these words to Moses and Moses gave them to Aaron and Aaron gave them to his sons and so it has continued from generation to generation. In some churches still today worshipers hear this blessing spoken over them.

Wherever the Israelites were in their journey, desert or Promised Land, and whenever they were in their journey, this generation or the next, the Lord met them there with his word of blessing. This God was in it for the long haul. He would travel with his children through space and time, offering a blessing in detail for every generation in every place they found themselves.

By sending Jesus to die on the cross, God has covered every devastating detail of our sin. Because of Christ's death and resurrection, nothing can ever separate you from God's love.

God, the maker of the heavens and the earth, the one who was there before you were born and the one who will meet you as you close your eyes in death, chooses to be with you now, in every detail of your journey. The one who put eyelashes on infants knows how to take care of you.

Heavenly Father, you have blessed every detail of my life. Help me to entrust all my days and all my ways to you. Amen.

NOTHING CAN EVER SEPARATE YOU FROM GOD'S LOVE.

> *This is how you are to bless the Israelites.*
> Numbers 6:23

When Aaron and his sons blessed the people, they raised their hands over them and spoke the words God had given. Raising one's hands was the traditional posture for prayer. But this time, something was different.

Instead of turning their palms up toward God, they turned them out toward the people. This blessing was not an act of prayer, asking favor from God, but an act of grace, bestowing God's favor upon his people. God's blessing was as abundant as the heavens above and as certain as the earth beneath. So whenever the priests blessed the people, they raised their arms to heaven and extended their hands over the earth.

Holding your hands in the air, however, can be tiring. Think of the last time you painted a ceiling or hung window blinds. You can hold your hands up for only so long before you need to bring them down.

Now, think about raising your hands in blessing. Loving the lovable is easy. When we like someone, we generously share our time and our talents with them. But put someone in front of us who is hard to love, and our arms quickly grow weary. When faced with a backbiting co-worker, the partner on the project who does poor work but claims great credit, or the Little League coach who knows little about coaching and less about children, we think of all of the reasons not to help. Our hands grow weary, our hearts harden, and instead of blessing, we curse.

God, however, never grows weary in bestowing his favor. As Jesus hung, dying on the cross, he opened the kingdom of heaven to a penitent thief. Even while taking his last earthly breaths, Jesus used his strength to bring salvation to others.

In that cross, God forgives our stinginess in sharing his blessings, and he invites us to live generously, blessing the world he has covered with his love. So love richly, bless freely, share God's favor with abandon! You are his, and you are blessed!

Almighty God, you have freely bestowed your blessings on this world. Bless me with divine generosity that I might share your mercy without measure. Amen.

YOU ARE HIS,
AND YOU ARE BLESSED.

During the next two days, think about being blessed and blessing.

BEING BLESSED: God has blessed you through particular people in your life. Name them and the ways in which they have been a blessing to you. Give God thanks for those blessings.

BLESSING: God has blessed you that you might be a blessing to others. Name the people God has placed into your life, and consider ways you can be a blessing to them. Ask God's guidance on your faithful service.

The LORD bless you and keep you.
Numbers 6:24

> *The LORD bless you and keep you.*
> Numbers 6:24

"It's amazing what you can hear, once you start listening," he said. My friend was talking about a recent camping trip. Early in the morning, he'd go out and sit on the edge of the lake and, as the world awakened, he'd listen. What he heard amazed him.

Scientists call it *sound refraction*. In the morning, the air near the surface of the lake is cooled by the water, but higher up, the air is warmed by the rising sun. This creates a thermal inversion.

Since the speed of sound is faster in warmer air, sounds rise from one shore in the early morning and bend over the lake in an arc of warm air. We hear sounds from a distant shore. Natural amplification.

God's words of blessing bring similar amazement. Spiritual amplification! Three times the priest calls out the name of the LORD, and each time the blessing extends a little bit longer. In Hebrew, the blessing grows. It amplifies from three to five to seven words.

The first word is *bless you*. Many words follow that one, and if you listen, what you hear will amaze you! Unconditional love. Forgiveness. Protection. Strength. God's blessing covers every aspect of life. In fact, the longer you listen, the more you will hear.

Unfortunately, we don't always take time to listen. We rise up early to get a head start on our work, and we stay up late to finish something before going to bed. Overwhelmed by work, we miss God's overwhelming blessing.

Yet God continues to bless. He speaks and invites us to listen. David's voice rises from a distant shore and guides our prayer today: "Let the morning bring me word of your unfailing love, for I have put my trust in you" (Psalm 143:8).

God's love never fails. Jesus died for our sins and rose again to bring us that sure and certain hope. This day, this morning, every morning for the rest of your life, your Savior will call out to you in blessing. He will awaken you to his mercies.

Father of all mercies, every morning you bring blessings known and unknown into our lives. Teach us to listen that we might know your bountiful, merciful work. Amen.

GOD CONTINUES TO BLESS.

> *The* LORD *bless you and keep you.*
> Numbers 6:24

His words were strange. I overheard him talking with a group of guys at a men's retreat. "Yeah, that accident was one of God's greatest blessings in my life," he said. He was speaking from a wheelchair.

His words struck me as strange, because *suffering* and *blessing* don't usually belong together. In our culture, we associate blessing with prosperity, with material possessions, with health and security. Here, however, sat a young man in a wheelchair calling himself blessed!

Having lost the power of his legs in an accident, he had not lost the power of God's Spirit. In fact, to hear him talk, his spiritual life had grown through suffering. Faith mattered. Relationships were more important now than they had been before. His reliance on God had increased.

Scholars used to think that the Hebrew word for "blessing" was associated with a word for "bended knee." They have since discovered there is not a connection. But although the words are not connected linguistically, spiritually they are.

God's blessing is known most fully not in bounty, but in his bended knee. In Jesus, God stoops down. He touches the lowliest places on earth and brings his blessing. Being born in a stable, washing his disciples' feet, dying on a cross, and rising from a borrowed tomb, Jesus enters the lowly places of our lives and fills them with his blessing. Because he has forgiven our sins and defeated the powers of Satan, nothing lies outside his power to bless.

In Jesus, the poor in spirit, the mourning, and the meek find blessing. The apostle Paul found even his famous "thorn" bringing him closer to God. Early Christians discovered spiritual wealth in their poverty and divine strength in their weakness.

Do you consider yourself blessed? If you look for God's blessing only in bounty, you may miss out on his most marvelous work. Consider the low times of your life—times of weakness, of suffering. Can you see a blessing?

If not, can you bring this to Jesus? The one who comes to you on bended knee will bring his touch of blessing.

Humble Lord, in bending your knee you blessed the lowly. Help me bring the low points of my life to you to find your blessing there. Amen.

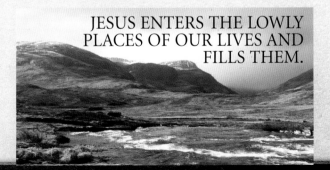

JESUS ENTERS THE LOWLY PLACES OF OUR LIVES AND FILLS THEM.

> *The LORD bless you and keep you.*
> Numbers 6:24

Wander. That's what the Israelites did for forty years in the wilderness. They wandered. Yet when you look at it more closely, they didn't so much wander as they followed. They followed the blessing of God.

Whenever the Israelites camped, God dwelt in their midst. He blessed the tabernacle with the cloud of his presence. When that cloud arose, Israel rose with it. Packing up tent and gathering children, they followed God in a pillar of cloud by day and a pillar of fire by night. He led them on a journey of blessing.

His leading continues today.

The last time the disciples saw Jesus, he was rising from earth into heaven. The one who had dwelt in their midst and blessed them by kneeling in service was rising from earth to bless them by ruling in heaven.

Risen from the dead, in his ascension Jesus publicly demonstrated his authority to rule in heaven and on earth (Matthew 28:18). Now he rules to lead you, forgiven and free from sin's guilt and power, on a journey of blessing.

Luke tells us that when Jesus ascended into heaven, his hands were raised in blessing (Luke 24:50). Because his arms are stretched out over the world, there is no place you can go to find yourself beyond God's blessing.

That's good news, because it's easy to feel like our life's journey consists of aimless wandering. Simply visiting family can take us across the country, and traveling for our jobs can take us across the globe. Yet wherever we go, God's blessing overshadows us. That's what it means for Jesus to rule over all things in blessing.

We may be traveling on vacation or off visiting family, we may be taking our son to a soccer game or our daughter to college, we may be rushing to a hospital or processing to a cemetery, but never, ever do we travel alone.

God's blessing covers all our journeys. He rose and ascended in blessing that we might rise and follow in faith.

Risen Lord, you ascended into heaven with your hands raised in blessing. Bless me now in my journeys. Take my worldly wanderings and make them a faithful following of you. Amen.

GOD'S BLESSING COVERS
ALL OUR JOURNEYS.

The LORD bless you and keep you.
Numbers 6:24

"Use the right tool for the job." That's a bit of worker's wisdom. It saves time, effort, and frustration. Sometimes, however, you have to be resourceful. You don't even know the right tool, much less have it, so you do the best you can.

For example, how do you protect someone you love? Your daughter goes to a party. What tool will guarantee her protection? Your wife is stressed out at work or your father's memory begins to fail. What tool do you pick up then?

Migrant shepherds in ancient Israel learned to be resourceful. Protecting a flock in the wilderness was not easy. Far from any village and faced with predators, shepherds would gather branches from thornbushes to create a "keep." Stacking the branches, they'd form an enclosure, a wall woven of thorns to protect the sheep. With sheep safely gathered, the shepherds would lie down in the doorway. They laid their own lives on the line—literally—as one last tool of protection.

As God's people journeyed through the wilderness, they camped far from any village and faced unknown dangers. Where could they go for protection?

In answer, God spoke words of blessing. Not only would God bless Israel, he would keep them. That is, he would shelter them, protect them, and defend them from their enemies, known and unknown.

Resourceful, God made water flow from rocks, the bread of angels fall from heaven, and flocks of quail fly in to feed his people. Most importantly, however, he would send his own Son to lay down his life for them.

After God had led Israel through the wilderness, brought them to the Promised Land, and led them into exile and back again, he sent his Son, Jesus, to live among them, to die for them, and, rising again, to create an eternal "keep."

When you or someone you love needs protection and you don't have the right tool, remember Jesus. He is the one who promises to keep us. Entrust your loved ones to his care. With all creation at his command, our resourceful God will keep them.

Protecting Savior, you keep us from all evil. Help me to entrust my life and my loved ones to your sheltering care. Amen.

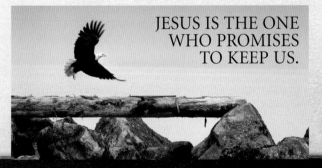

JESUS IS THE ONE WHO PROMISES TO KEEP US.

> *The LORD bless you and keep you.*
> Numbers 6:24

There he stood, on the mountain, overlooking the people of Israel. Balaam saw them but could not curse them.

He would be paid good money to curse them. It was in his best interest to curse them. But every time he opened his mouth, he blessed rather than cursed.

As a prophet, Balaam knew the power of divination. His tongue had tasted the language of gods. Yet when the king of Moab hired him to curse the people of Israel, Balaam encountered a god unlike any other. He met the one true God—the LORD, who would "bless and keep" his people.

Balaam's tongue was tied, his spirit was bound, so he blessed rather than cursed. God turned Balaam's curse into a blessing. That's what it means for the Lord to bless and keep his people.

Shepherds often made "keeps" for their flock out of thornbushes. The thorns, sharp and painful, would keep the predators out and the sheep in. Shepherds took that which was painful and used it for good.

God does this, as well. He did it for ancient Israel. In Genesis, when Joseph was sold into slavery, God used evil for good. He raised Joseph to rule over Egypt, saving all Egypt and his chosen, covenant people, too, from starvation.

God did this for the early church. In Acts, when believers were scattered by the pain of persecution, God used evil for good. Those who were scattered took the message of salvation to the ends of the earth.

God does this for you, too! Consider the death and resurrection of Jesus Christ. God takes the cross, an instrument of punishment, and uses it for good—the forgiveness of your sins.

No one is loved by everyone in this world. We all know "Balaams" who would rather curse than bless us. How do we deal with them? Retaliate? Run?

Jesus says, "Love your enemies" and "Turn the other cheek" (Matthew 5:38–48). Why? Because Jesus knows God's protection turns curses into blessings. His love turns enemies into friends.

Blessed Savior, when others curse, you bless. You turn even their curses into blessings. Strengthen me when faced with enemies, so that I trust your blessing and share your life-giving love. Amen.

GOD TAKES THE CROSS AND USES IT FOR GOOD.

During the next two days, think about God blessing and keeping you.

GOD'S BLESSING: God has stooped down to bless you in the low points of your life, and he rises to lead you in the ways of his blessing. Bring your past and your future before God, asking for his blessing.

GOD'S KEEPING: God protects you and your loved ones, turning evil into good. Look for his keeping in your life. Bring your thanks and your concerns before God in prayer.

The LORD make his face shine upon you
and be gracious to you.
Numbers 6:25

> *The LORD make his face shine upon you.*
> Numbers 6:25

"He didn't even look at me."

My friend always had a difficult relationship with his father. Nothing he did was ever good enough. When he made the basketball team, his dad asked why he wasn't a starter. When he got into college, his dad muttered, "Goes to show they'll take anyone these days."

Now, with worries about his company downsizing, my friend went to talk to his father. But his dad just kept watching TV. Whether my friend was winning in basketball or losing in life, it didn't matter. His dad was never there for him. To use biblical language, his dad hid his face.

You know how painful that can be. You need support and turn to others, but they turn away. They hide their face.

And God . . . what happens when you turn to him? In this blessing, God promises never to hide his face from you. Whether you have disappointed him in your marriage, angered your kids, or misused your friends, God will not look away. He sees your sin, but he forgives you. He makes his face to shine on you and supports you no matter what.

God does all of this because of the day Jesus carried all your sin to his cross. The sky darkened that day, as creation closed its eyes and God the Father looked away. God hid his face from his Son. On that day, God looked away from your sin forever, and because of Jesus he promises always to look with favor on you.

What does that mean?

Well, for my friend, it means that he remains in relationship with a dad who does not love him. Why? Because he knows that his heavenly Father does.

Years of trying to get his father's approval and of lashing out in anger are over. My friend is patient and loving toward someone who does not love him, because he knows his heavenly Father is patient and loving toward him. Forever.

Heavenly Father, you hid your face from Jesus on the cross so that you might always look on me in love. Give me confidence in that love and forgiveness, so I may be patient and strong even when I face those who are unloving. Amen.

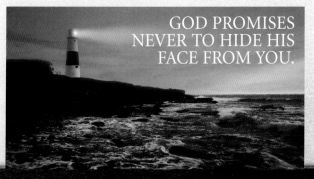

GOD PROMISES NEVER TO HIDE HIS FACE FROM YOU.

> *The LORD make his face shine upon you.*
> Numbers 6:25

After the Super Bowl, World Series, or Stanley Cup, you see it—a celebration to end all celebrations. The athletes have fought hard and won. Their bodies are bruised and battered. But for a moment, such suffering doesn't matter. They enter the joy of victory.

While it wasn't a Super Bowl party, the people of the Old Testament had something similar. They poured olive oil on a person's head in celebration. They called it anointing. It set a person apart for sacred service. People would look to the person shining with oil to see what God would do.

The psalmist describes such a moment: "Precious oil poured on the head, running down on the beard, running down on Aaron's beard, down upon the collar of his robes" (Psalm 133:2). Imagine Aaron's head and face at this moment. They would actually shine, drenched in God's anointing.

This vision is rare. You don't win the Super Bowl every day. Most of our days are ordinary. We go about life as best we can, struggling on in the gruel of the game.

An irate customer, a backstabbing co-worker—their voices shout at us from the sidelines, even after we leave work for the day. Kids scream as they run down the hallway, and the TV won't drown out the noise. Arguments soon follow. We raise our voices, snapping in anger. Bruised and battered, we wonder if we'll make it through the game.

That's when it comes—a small voice, calm and confident: "The LORD make his face shine upon you." This voice brings blessing. It lifts our eyes from the field of battle. We look up and see a face. Jesus' face. Shining. In victory.

God the Father anointed his Son to fight with sin, and he has won for you the victory. His face now shines upon you.

Bruised and battered though you may be, you are his. And he promises to work in all things for your good, to bring you through every struggle to that day when you will join the victory celebration that never ends.

Jesus, anointed by God, look on me in my daily struggles. Remind me of your love so that I may celebrate your victory. Amen.

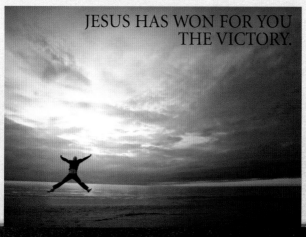

JESUS HAS WON FOR YOU THE VICTORY.

> *The LORD . . . be gracious to you.*
> Numbers 6:25

Men aren't often accused of grace. When you write your resume, you probably don't use words like *gracious* or *graceful. Leadership, courage, strength, productivity*—these are the words we hope others use when they describe us. And yet, there is a godly graciousness for men.

A soldier holds his M16A2. Under the pressure of real combat, his senses are sharp. He manages his breathing and position so he doesn't disturb the sight system alignment. He makes split-second decisions: is that figure civilian or enemy? And his work saves lives.

What do you call this ability to use one's skill and strength for good at a critical time? *Grace under pressure.*

Being gracious is not about social niceties or using the right fork at the dinner table. It's about being able to harness your strength and use it for good while your surroundings pressure you to lose control. We see it on the battlefield when soldiers do their duty; we see it on the sports field when players make that critical play; and God desires that others see it in our lives.

As men of God, we live under pressure. How do you control your sex drive when everything around you, from TV to the Internet, encourages you to be unfaithful? How do you control your ambition, when there's pressure at work to do anything to get ahead?

It's easy to use our power for evil. Where do we go for strength to do good? David writes, "It is God who arms me with strength. . . . He trains my hands for battle" (Psalm 18:32–34). God's grace doesn't make you a wimp. It gives you strength—the strength of his love.

Consider the death of Jesus. When mocked and pressured to come down from the cross, Jesus could have called down an army of avenging angels. Instead, he hung there. Nails didn't hold him to the cross. Graciousness did. He used his strength in love to die for you, to bring you forgiveness and life.

That's grace under pressure.

Gracious Lord, when I'm under pressure, teach me to love that which is good, to fight that which is evil, and to work for that which is godly, drawing my strength from you. Amen.

HE USED HIS STRENGTH
IN LOVE TO DIE FOR YOU.

> *The LORD . . . be gracious to you.*
> Numbers 6:25

My friend has a great way of getting to the heart of the matter. Even if I haven't seen her for years, before long, we will be standing at the intersection of faith and life, talking about what really matters.

You know how it is when you haven't seen someone for a long time. You race along, catching one another up on the basic details. Rarely do you delve into what's really important. You promise to get back together soon, but it seldom happens.

My friend, however, has a way of cutting through the small talk. She simply looks at me and says, "So . . . what are you praying about?"

Her question hangs in the air.

I take a deep breath and think about my most recent prayers. When I begin to answer, I find myself talking about what matters most to me.

That's how prayer is. When we pray, we bring before God the core issues. A recent storm in our marriage. A mother's failing memory. A son's increasing distance. An addiction we can't quite kill. We lift to God even the burdens we cannot quite put into words.

It's always been this way. As you read the psalms, you overhear holy, heartfelt prayer. David cries out after being caught in adultery. Israel tries to put into words her degrading suffering in captivity.

Why such radical honesty in prayer? Part of the answer lies in this blessing. These words, like my friend's question, lead us into radical, holy, heartfelt prayer.

Of the times the Old Testament uses the word *gracious* to describe God, over half occur in the psalms. The Lord's promise to be gracious opened the hearts of his people. They called upon him to hear and to heal, to see and to strengthen, to raise up and to redeem—all because he promised to be gracious. Prayer is the echo of God's graciousness in the human heart.

When Jesus died for you, he loved you radically. No sin now lies beyond his forgiveness, no situation beyond his love. So God's grace, promised to you in this blessing, invites your radical prayer. Bring anything and everything to God.

Radical Lord, let your grace inspire me to holy, heartfelt prayer. Amen.

JESUS LOVES YOU RADICALLY.

> *The law was given through Moses; grace
> and truth came through Jesus Christ.*
> John 1:17

Some words start a lifetime. These words are rare. You
don't hear them every day. Once spoken, however, they
change everything.

"I do," he said, standing there with a goofy grin on his face.
The wedding service seemed silly to him. All of the dresses
and tuxes, flowers and pictures. He just wanted it to be
over so they could return to life as normal. But life would
not be normal. Life had changed. He had promised to be
there for one woman for one lifetime, for richer, for
poorer, in sickness, and in health. Those words, spoken so
quickly, would take a lifetime to understand.

"It's a boy." He wasn't able to make the doctor's
appointment, so his wife shared the news over the phone.
He stood there, in line for coffee at Chicago O'Hare, and
he couldn't believe that everyone just walked by him. Life
had changed. Couldn't they tell? He was going to have a
son. Suddenly, though in an airport, in line for coffee, far
from anyone he knew, those words brought him close to
home. In his heart, he promised to be there for his wife
and son.

Some words start a lifetime, and that's how it is with these
words of blessing. They start a lifetime of grace. God's
grace—not for one person, but for all people. Not for one

generation, but for all generations. Not only for this world, but also for the next. God's blessing spans eternity with his life-giving love.

Aaron spoke to Israel, "The LORD . . . be gracious to you" (Numbers 6:25). Paul spoke to the churches, "The grace of the Lord Jesus Christ . . . be with you all" (2 Corinthians 13:14). Pastors speak these words. Today. To you.

At the heart of this blessing is the life of God's own Son, Jesus Christ. He came into this world to bring his Father's grace to you. He gave his life that you might live—eternally. He rose that you might rise in love and forgiveness to share his blessing, his grace, with others.

Lord, your words have changed my life. Teach me now to live for you. Amen.

GOD'S BLESSING SPANS ETERNITY.

During the next two days, let God's blessing inspire your prayer. His face is turned toward you and his grace spans your lifetime.

Bring before him . . .

- **YOUR PAST:** Name people and places of your life, asking God to bless how these have formed you.

- **YOUR PRESENT:** Name people God has placed in your life, asking him to share his blessing with them through you.

- **YOUR FUTURE:** Name the work of God's church in the world, asking God to bring his mission to fruition through you.

The LORD turn his face toward you
and give you peace.
Numbers 6:26

> *The LORD turn his face toward you.*
> Numbers 6:26

I still remember the smile on their faces. I was in sixth grade and had a trumpet solo in the school play. The stage darkened, a spotlight illuminated the American flag, and I played the national anthem.

Poorly.

Looking back now, I'd have to say very poorly. The tempo was off, the notes were off, and the only thing consistent was the light on the flag.

After the play, I was sure my parents would be disappointed in me. All those weeks practicing the national anthem in the basement. For what? So I could put everyone else through the pain? I was sure they would be disappointed, and I was ashamed.

But when I came down the hall, I saw them both smile. They smiled at me. I may not have played well, but they were still proud. Proud that I played at all and happy that I was their son.

We can so easily think that God's favor depends upon our work for him. If we do well, he loves us. If we do poorly, he doesn't. Those who think they do well become proud of their work, certain God loves them. Those who struggle with God's will struggle also with God's love and wonder if they even belong.

Certainly God delights in a job well done. He calls us to work for him in this world, he supports us in our efforts, and he rejoices in what we do. But his love does not depend on that.

His love is like that of my parents. While your work isn't perfect, that does not change God's love for you. The Lord makes his face shine on you, not because of your work but because of his Son.

Jesus did the will of his Father perfectly. He died on the cross to forgive your sins. Because of Jesus, God the Father claims you as his son. Your faults are forgiven, and he promises to love and forgive, to strengthen and support you forever. What amazing love! Your heavenly Father's favor.

Heavenly Father, I bring before you all my work. Bless it as you bless me with your amazing love. Amen.

THE LORD MAKES HIS FACE SHINE ON YOU.

> *The LORD turn his face toward you.*
> Numbers 6:26

People did not overlook Jairus. He was a synagogue ruler. Crowds came to him. They respected him. They followed him. Now he had gone to Jesus for help because of his daughter. When he looked at her, he no longer saw his little girl. He no longer saw the woman she would be. Instead, he saw what all will be. Dead.

She was sick and dying and desperately needed help. Although it was controversial and humiliating, he came to this traveling teacher and asked him to come to his home. Jesus agreed.

But a crowd surrounded Jesus. Someone reached through to touch him, grabbing a gift of healing. Jesus stopped moving. "Who touched me?" he asked. With a crowd like this, what did it matter? Jairus needed Jesus to come to his house. But Jesus just stood there.

At that moment, Jairus was lost in the crowd. Why should Jesus come with him? What was he to Jesus? Jairus feared he was just one more need in one more town on one more day of Jesus' ministry.

What do you bring before Jesus today? A rocky marriage . . . a broken promise . . . a wayward son? Whatever you bring, you don't want to be lost in the crowd. Yet, you see the world around you. So many faces. So much need. Why should God care about you?

But God does care! Listen to this blessing. He has "[turned] his face toward you." God's love is personal. He looks at every face, numbers every hair, blesses every life. When Jesus died on the cross, he did so for every sin for every person for all time.

You cannot be lost in the crowd. God saw you, died for you, and promises to turn his face toward you forever.

The voice of Jesus breaks through the crowd. He speaks to Jairus: "Don't be afraid; just believe, and she will be healed" (Luke 8:50).

Today, God's voice breaks through the crowded confusion you face. He speaks to you: "You are mine and you are loved. I have turned my face toward you."

Watchful Savior, I bring you all my needs, because you have turned your face toward me. Amen.

GOD'S LOVE IS PERSONAL.

> *The LORD . . . give you peace.*
> Numbers 6:26

When Jesus was born, God peeled back a corner of the sky. The invisible suddenly became visible. Shepherds in the fields saw angels in the sky, and choirs in heaven sang of "peace on earth."

After that night, however, peace was harder to find. Herod slaughtered the infants in Bethlehem, John the Baptizer suffered imprisonment, and people wondered, "Where is God's peace?"

Jesus himself shocked followers with his words: "Do not suppose that I have come to bring peace to the earth. I did not come to bring peace, but a sword. For I have come to turn 'a man against his father, a daughter against her mother'" (Matthew 10:34–35).

What does Jesus mean? Were the angels wrong? Doesn't God's blessing bring peace?

The angels weren't wrong. They just saw more than we are able to see. They looked deep into the heart of God and sang of a peace different from that of this world. God's peace. In this world, people associate peace with tolerance. Our world lives in peace by tolerating sin. That's how the world avoids conflict.

In his ministry, however, Jesus never tolerated evil. He named it, he fought it, and he died to forgive it. His teachings divide truth from error, right from wrong, love from hate, good from evil, life from death. He did it then, and he does it now.

This is the peace of salvation, the peace that Jesus brings. Not the absence of conflict, but the presence of love in the midst of conflict. The work of a Savior, fighting evil to bring the forgiveness of sin.

Faith in Jesus brings conflict in this world. It will set you at odds with others; your beliefs may offend co-workers, friends, even family. Does the presence of conflict mean the absence of peace? Has God stopped blessing?

No!

To God, some things are still worth fighting for—goodness, truth, life, salvation . . . you! Jesus did not come to tolerate sin but to fight it and to forgive it. Though faith creates conflict, Jesus brings a peace that saves the world.

Jesus, when faith in you brings conflict in my life, teach me to trust your peace that saves the world. Amen.

TO GOD, SOME THINGS ARE
STILL WORTH FIGHTING FOR.

> *The LORD . . . give you peace.*
> Numbers 6:26

We tend to associate peace with quiet. Sometimes, however, quiet is the enemy of peace.

Jeremiah was a prophet called by God to speak difficult words to difficult people in difficult times. His words brought him beatings and imprisonment. Yet he spoke. Why? Well, let him explain:

> *If I say, "I will not mention him or speak any more in his name," his word is in my heart like a fire, a fire shut up in my bones. I am weary of holding it in; indeed, I cannot.*
> Jeremiah 20:9

God's Word could not be silenced. When Jeremiah tried to hold it in, it tore him apart. So, he spoke. The words were hard, yet Jeremiah spoke them. Why? Because he knew that in difficult times, among difficult people, God's Word alone brings peace.

What is the word that God has given you to say? You may not speak to kings. You may speak only to a child. But what is that word?

People tend to think of men as unexpressive. "He's a man of few words," they say. But there's a difference between being quiet and being a coward. Sometimes God calls us to speak difficult words, yet words that bring peace.

It could be a word of direction to a wayward child, a word of reconciliation to your estranged father, a word of apology to the woman you promised to love. Difficult words in difficult times among difficult people. Yet words that bring peace.

In Jesus, God spoke the most difficult word of all: "I forgive you." When faced with disciples who fled him, denied him, and now cowered in fear, Jesus spoke that difficult word: "Peace be with you" (John 20:19). He forgave them and sent them into the world with his Word of peace.

God's peace comes in the midst of conflicts, broken relationships, job-related stress. This peace is not easy. These words are hard to say. But men of God have a word from God and the courage to say it. We speak in difficult times and, in speaking, discover the God who brings peace.

Lord, give me the courage to speak your Word, so that in the midst of trouble you might bring peace. Amen.

DISCOVER THE GOD
WHO BRINGS PEACE.

> *The LORD . . . give you peace.*
> Numbers 6:26

Most of the day, you've been sitting in the hospital waiting room. Your father is dying, and now your daughter is falling asleep.

She's been good today. A hospital on Saturday afternoon is no place for a child. Too much beyond her understanding—strange machines and a grandfather who no longer speaks. "Is he sleeping?" she asks. You nod your head in a lie. "Then he'll feel better," she says and skips away.

Now, she can't find a good place to sleep. The chairs are hard. So she cuddles close to you. Soon, she lies down, at rest in your lap as your dad dies in the other room.

Strange, how your presence brings her peace. You doubt you make a good pillow. She's too big to hold and her arm, awkwardly placed, has to hurt. But the warmth of your body, your breathing, your presence—these things bring her peace.

So, too, with God. His presence brings peace.

The night when he was betrayed, Jesus spoke to his disciples. He told them about the prince of this world, the hour of darkness. They did not understand. Soon, they were lost in painful confusion. Betrayal. Mockery. Crucifixion.

But Jesus had said, "I have told you these things, so that in me you may have peace. In this world you will have trouble. But take heart! I have overcome the world" (John 16:33).

Jesus gave his disciples peace, not by taking them out of this world, but by coming into it himself. In him, they saw God's love: the Father sending his Son to die for all sinners and the Son willingly dying and rising to give life to all who believe. In his life, his death, and his resurrection, we know the loving presence of God.

In Jesus, we have peace.

Not because we understand all that is going on. We are like children in a hospital waiting room—so much of the pain and perplexity of this world lies beyond our understanding.

But in Jesus we have peace because in Jesus we have the presence of God. Rest in peace in the presence of Jesus. In him, you are loved.

Jesus, let your presence bring me peace. Amen.

WE KNOW THE LOVING PRESENCE OF GOD.

During the next two days, contemplate God's favor and peace.

GOD'S FAVOR: Name the ways, great and small, in which God has shown his personal love for you.

GOD'S PEACE: Consider any conflict in your life and in the lives of those you love. How can you bring God's Word into these situations and bear his presence among these people that others may know God's peace?

So they will put my name on the Israelites, and I will bless them.
Numbers 6:27

> *So they will put my name on the*
> *Israelites, and I will bless them.*
> Numbers 6:27

How long does God's blessing last? Is it like gas in your car, needing constant refilling? Or more like the beating of your heart—once begun, lasting a lifetime?

In ancient Israel, the priests spoke this blessing in times of worship. Blessing happened repeatedly. This could make God's blessing look like gas in a car, needing constant refilling. But notice how the passage ends: "So they will put my name on the Israelites."

Being blessed is being named.

How often do parents name their children? While they may repeat their names again and again, children are named only once. Their names never wear out. So, too, for God's blessing. When God's priest blessed, he put God's name upon the people. Wherever they went, whatever they did, they bore God's name. They remained his treasured possession.

Why, then, the repetition? Not because God's blessing wears out or needs refilling, but to reveal something about God. God is eternally blessing! It's easy to forget this. Sometimes, it can seem like God's blessings fade away. Life changes. Difficulties arise. We make stupid decisions and we wonder, "Is God still blessing? After all I've done, can God still bless . . . even this?"

In Jesus, God gives us his answer: Yes!

When Jesus was crucified, he died under God's curse for our sin. All God's judgment against all our sin lies buried with him. He died cursed, but he rose blessed. Blessed by God to be the source of your eternal blessing. Nothing can now separate you from God's love. Jesus lives, and you are blessed for life.

God wanted Israel to know that he was eternally blessing, so the priest put God's name on the people again and again.

God wants you to know the same.

You matter to God. He placed his name on you. Once for life. Eternally. Regardless of what happens in this world, God's heart beats with an eternal love. He knows you, sees you, cares for you. You are his child, bearing his name, and he is your God, blessing you always.

Eternal God, eternally blessing, teach me to trust that wherever I go, whatever I do, you have put your name on me. I am yours. Amen.

GOD'S HEART BEATS WITH AN ETERNAL LOVE.

> *So they will put my name on the*
> *Israelites, and I will bless them.*
> Numbers 6:27

You couldn't miss him as he walked into the gym. His T-shirt announced his presence. "THINK YOU'RE STRONG?" it said. With bold letters, he challenged everyone he met.

Looking at him, you wouldn't say you were strong. He was a big guy. He could lift a lot of weight. With a gym bag over his shoulder, he was ready to prove just how strong he could be. But then, he walked by . . . and everything changed.

On the back of his T-shirt was a completely different picture. There was Jesus, head crowned with thorns, arms spread out as if he were doing a push-up, lifting himself from the earth, with a bloody cross on his back.

"LIFT THIS!" it said. Think you're strong? Lift this cross . . . take this burden . . . carry the sins of the world on your back.

While this guy was strong, he knew someone stronger. Jesus. His Savior. The one who carried the weight of sin to the cross and carries the power of forgiveness to the world. As this guy walked into the gym, he didn't announce his presence. He announced the presence of Jesus. In a simple way, he shared with the world the story of Jesus, whose strong love saved him from sin.

"So they will put my name on the Israelites," God said. As the priest raised his hands and spoke this blessing, he marked God's people.

Some in Israel long ago made that mark visible. They took these words, inscribed them on silver, rolled that silver into scrolls, and wore the scrolls. Archaeologists sometimes find these scrolls in tombs. In life and in death, God's people knew who they were. Holy. Blessed. Marked by God.

The same is true for you.

In Jesus and his cross, God marked you with his love. Some Christians wear T-shirts, others wear crosses, others simply carry this mark in their words and their work in the world. All, however, know God has marked them. They are his people. Holy. Blessed.

Jesus, in your wounds I see the marks of your strong love. Give me strength to share your love with the world. Amen.

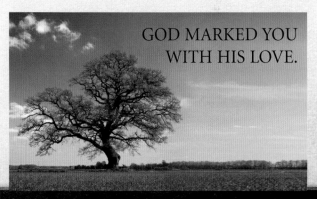

GOD MARKED YOU WITH HIS LOVE.

> *So they will put my name on the*
> *Israelites, and I will bless them.*
> Numbers 6:27

Some funeral homes want men to prearrange their funerals. So they advertise. Were the advertisers appealing to women, they might make an emotional argument. They could depict prearrangement as one last kind gesture, a beautiful way to help your loved ones through the difficulties of grief.

But they are speaking to men. So they ask a simple question. "Do you remember what your kids got you for your birthday last year?" They pause. You think of that tie. "Do you really want them planning your funeral?"

Leaving things to chance can lead to disaster. Take control over what will happen. Some things are that important. That's what the ad implies.

In this text, God leaves nothing to chance. He takes control of your future. It's that important to him. In the Hebrew, the first person pronoun is emphatic. "I, *even I*, will bless them," he says. God wants his people to know that he, himself, will do this blessing. The priests speak the words, but God will do the work.

God does not merely wish a blessing in your direction. Blessing you is not something he may get around to doing. Sometime. No. This is certain! God will do it.

Look around at the world—so much uncertainty. Health. Employment. Family. Home. Look into your heart—uncertainty increases. Who has the strength? Our desires, our will can get out of control.

Yet God refuses to let go of his desire, his will, his longing to bless you. So God reveals his control.

God the Father sends his Son, Jesus, to live, die, and rise for you. Before Jesus died, he named you God's child in his will. This was his new testament. When he died, Jesus made God's love certain. God forgives you your sin and fills your life with his blessing.

Our world is complex and uncertain. So much of life lies outside our control. One thing, however, we know for sure. God will bless you. Jesus died to make that promise certain for you.

Heavenly Father, you yourself have planned my blessing. When so much of life is out of my control, teach me to live in the certainty of your love. Amen.

GOD LEAVES NOTHING TO CHANCE.

> *So they will put my name on the*
> *Israelites, and I will bless them.*
> Numbers 6:27

If you stare into the light and then look away, what do you see? Even though you look at the ground or a loved one's face, for a brief moment, you can still see the light. Scientists call this an afterimage—a ghost image that haunts your vision after the original object is no longer there.

One wonders whether the disciples had an afterimage following Jesus' ascension.

Jesus had led them up the Mount of Olives, raised his hands in blessing, and ascended into heaven. The disciples stood there, on the mountain, staring up into the sky. They needed angel voices to call them back to their senses: "Why do you stand here looking into the sky?" (Acts 1:11). Only then did the disciples look away.

What did they see in that moment? Was there an afterimage of grace when they looked out upon the world? Scripture does not speak of afterimages or optical illusions, but it does reveal the reality of God's grace.

When Jesus ascended into heaven, he revealed his victory over sin, death, and the power of the devil. Jesus now rules over all. Eternally. He blesses for life. Nothing can take his people out of his hands.

Yet, Jesus blesses for life in another way, as well. Jesus blesses his disciples for life in this world.

When the disciples turned to look at the world, it had not changed. It was still a fallen world. Now, however, everywhere they looked, they saw their Savior, his hands raised in blessing. They saw Jesus bringing life, peace, and favor through their work in the world.

What about you? In Jesus, God has blessed you for life. Eternal life, yes. But also life in this world. Look around. Can you see Jesus, raising his hands in blessing over the moments of your life?

He's there when you spend an afternoon with your child. He's there during overtime at work. He's there in daily conversation with friends. And he brings his grace, his favor, his blessing, through you into his world.

Jesus, when you left this world, your hands were raised in blessing. Teach me to see you now, your hands upraised and blessing still. Amen.

IN JESUS, GOD HAS BLESSED YOU FOR LIFE.

> *So they will put my name on the*
> *Israelites, and I will bless them.*
> Numbers 6:27

When wandering in the wilderness, Israel had no home. No walled cities declared who they were. No villages marked their place on any map.

But God commanded them to build a portable tabernacle, a "tent of meeting." They carried this holy place with them wherever they went. And God came to dwell in it. He lived among his people, leading them with his presence.

Scripture records that Moses and Aaron often went into the tent, entering the presence of God. "When they came out, they blessed the people; and the glory of the LORD appeared" (Leviticus 9:23).

That's the way it is with the glory of the Lord. God reveals his glory by living with his people, leading us, and blessing us wherever we go.

Consider how John describes God coming among us in Jesus. He writes that "the Word became flesh and made his dwelling among us"; there, we saw "his glory" (John 1:14). The word for "dwelling" is *tented*. Jesus "tabernacled" among us.

Jesus built no city on earth. He fought for no earthly kingdom. He traveled deep into the palaces of kings and out into the pastures of shepherds. He walked in the halls of the temple and over the hills of Galilee. He ate in the houses of sinners and hung on the cross with thieves.

Jesus "tented" among us so that we could see the glory of the Lord. God lived in our midst, leading us with his presence, blessing us with forgiveness. This is God's glory—loving and saving sinners. Jesus brought salvation to the ends of the earth, and now he brings forgiveness and life everlasting to you.

For the past five weeks, you have seen that God lives with you. God leads you. God blesses you. It is his glory to bless and forgive you. Now and always. Here and everywhere. To the ends of the earth and to the end of time.

Be blessed!

Lord, live with me, and I will be strong. Lead me, and I will follow. Bless me, and I will share your boundless blessing with the world. Amen.

THIS IS GOD'S GLORY—LOVING AND SAVING SINNERS.

Prayerfully consider how you have been blessed for life:

God's blessing is present for all of your life.

LOOK AROUND: How can you see his blessing in your past? How is God blessing you right now, in the present? How can you live as one confident of God's blessing in the future?

God's blessing is present that you might have a full life.

LOOK AHEAD: How does God's blessing lead you into a life of thankfulness? of love toward God? of service toward others?

The LORD said to Moses, "Tell Aaron
and his sons, 'This is how you are to
bless the Israelites. Say to them:

" ' "The LORD bless you
and keep you;
the LORD make his face shine upon you
and be gracious to you;
the LORD turn his face toward you
and give you peace." '

"So they will put my name on the
Israelites, and I will bless them."
Numbers 6:22–27

If this book has made a difference in your life
or if you have simply enjoyed it, we would like
to hear from you. Your words will encourage us!
If you have suggestions for us to consider as
we create books like this in the future,
please send those, too.
You can reach us at:

Editorial Manager, Department MBL9HC
CTA, Inc.
PO Box 1205
Fenton, MO 63026-1205

or by e-mail at editor@CTAinc.com.
Please include the subject line: MBL9HC.